JN

HALLOWEEN

D. J. HERDA

HALLOWEEN

FRANKLIN WATTS

New York / London / Toronto / Sydney / 1983

A FIRST BOOK

Illustrations by Anne Canevari Green

Photographs courtesy of:
Religious News Service: opp. page 1, 11, 16, 26;
Bettmann Archive: pp. 6, 55;
The New York Public Library: pp. 18, 34, 50, 52;
Elizabeth McDonald: p. 30;
State Historical Society of Wisconsin: pp. 33

Library of Congress Cataloging in Publication Data

Herda, D. J., 1948-
Halloween.

(A First book)
Includes index.
Summary: Describes the origin and development
of Halloween, its traditions and celebrations,
and provides instructions for making costumes
and having a Halloween party.
1. Halloween—Juvenile literature. [1. Halloween]
I. Green, Anne Canevari, ill, II. Title.
GT4965.H38 1983   394.2'683   82-16025
ISBN 0-531-04527-7

CONTENTS

1

HOW HALLOWEEN BEGAN

Ghosts, goblins, and witches. Warlocks, fairies, and demons. There is no other holiday quite like Halloween. It's a peculiar mix of pagan customs, religious traditions, and frightening superstitions.

The earliest Halloween celebrations took place among the Celts, who lived more than 2,000 years ago in what is now England, Ireland, Scotland, Wales, and northern France. The Celtic order of Druids (priests) used to honor Samhain, the lord of the dead, on the evening of October 31 and the day of November 1. According to ancient Celtic legend, Samhain could control the spirits of the dead. He could allow them to rest peacefully or spur them into wild and frenzied activity.

The Celts also believed that on October 31, Samhain assembled the souls of all those who had died during the previous year. This was the Vigil of Samhain. To pay for their sins, these souls were put into the bodies of animals. The greater a person's sins, the lower the animal into which his or her soul was placed. All sorts of goblins, spirits, and fairies were thought to roam the earth during the Vigil of Samhain.

In addition to worshiping Samhain, the Celts also worshiped their own sun god. They believed that the sun, as the ripener of grain, was their greatest friend. Without the sun, there would be no food, and the people would starve. So, once the summer's harvest was safely stored, the Celts tried to help strengthen the sun god for the coming battle with the darkness and cold of winter. To do this they offered animal sacrifices to the sun on November 1, the Celtic New Year.

In nearby Rome, a festival honoring the goddess Pomona was also held around November 1. Pomona was the mistress of fruits and gardens. The Romans pictured Pomona as a beautiful young maiden, her arms filled with fruit and a crown of apples on her head. To thank Pomona for good harvests, the Romans laid out apples and nuts in her honor. Then they played various games, held races, and celebrated throughout the day and night.

When the Romans conquered the Gauls, a Celtic people in what is now France, they brought their customs with them. Soon the Roman festival honoring Pomona and the Celtic Vigil of Samhain were both held at the time we now celebrate Halloween. The result was a great fall holiday that mixed customs from two cultures.

Later, during the Middle Ages, witchcraft emerged as an organized cult opposed to the Roman Catholic Church. Halloween became known as the Night of the Witch. It was then, according to superstition, that the devil and all of his followers—witches, warlocks (male witches), and demons—gathered. They would mock the coming of the Church's festival of All Saints' Day on November 1 by performing unholy acts.

In Germany, these demons supposedly met at a mountain called the Brocken. In Sweden, they assembled at the Blocksberg. In France, they reveled in the Forest of Ardennes. In England, any old church, ruined abbey, or monument served as their meeting place.

The Church had earlier established November 1 as All Saints', or All Hallows', Day. On that day, the saints who had no church holiday of their own were honored. As with many Church holidays, November 1 was chosen because it was already the date of a pagan celebration. The Church leaders hoped that, by making November 1 a religious ceremony, the pagan rituals that had survived over the centuries would be forgotten.

As much as the early Church leaders wished the pagan rituals of Pomona Day and the Vigil of Samhain would disappear, they did not. People around the world continued pagan celebrations on the evening before All Hallows. It became known as All Hallows Even. While All Hallows was a day for religious thought and church services, All Hallows Even was a night for magic and superstition. As time went on, the name All Hallows Even was shortened to Hallowe'en. Then it became Halloween.

Halloween combined many of the religious customs from All Saints' Day and All Souls' Day (celebrated on November 2 in memory of the dead) and the pagan customs of Pomona Day and the Vigil of Samhain. From All Saints' and All Souls' days came the traditional honoring of the dead and their spirits. From Pomona Day came apples, nuts, and other symbols of the harvest. And from the Vigil of Samhain came goblins, fortune-telling, magic, black cats, and evil spirits.

Today, Halloween is basically a secular (nonreligious) holiday. It's a time to have fun and make fun of superstitions like witches, ghosts, and goblins. Children dress in costumes, such as elves, fairies, ghosts, witches, and other fantastic creatures. It's a special time of year—a time to let your imagination go. What if there really were such things as ghosts, goblins, and witches? What if? What if?

2

HALLOWEEN AROUND THE WORLD

As we have seen, many of the Halloween legends and customs of today have come from the Celts. One centuries-old tradition which is still celebrated in parts of Europe is the great bonfire of the Vigil of Samhain.

The pagan Celts believed that evil spirits lurked about as the sun god grew pale and Samhain, lord of the dead, grew stronger. By lighting great bonfires on the hillsides, they hoped to scare these spirits away. Also on this important day, all the cooking fires were extinguished in the kitchens around the land. New fires were then lit from the great bonfire to honor the coming new year.

To this day, many of those who live in the countryside of Scotland and Ireland—where the Druid religion lasted longer than anywhere else in the Celtic region—build huge bonfires. When the last fires die out, the people race each other down the hills shouting, "The Devil gets the last one down!"

Snap Apple Night in England

Another ancient Celtic Halloween custom is still celebrated. The countryfolk lace their pitchforks with dry straw and set the straw on fire. Then, waving the pitchforks in the air, the people warn all witches to leave the area. If any witches fly too low, the flaming pitchforks are supposed to singe their evil brooms and send the witches scurrying elsewhere.

The people of Wales, like those of Ireland and Scotland, also built Halloween fires on the Vigil of Samhain. But their celebration was much more somber. Each family member wrote his or her name on a white stone and threw it into the fire. Then the family marched around the fire, praying for good fortune. In the morning, after the fire had died out, each family member sifted the ashes in search of his or her stone. If a stone was missing, it meant that the spirits would call the soul of that person during the coming year.

In England, Halloween was nicknamed *Nutcrack Night* or *Snap Apple Night*. Families sat before great fires in the hearth, roasting nuts and eating apples. They told stories and played holiday games. It was an evening of great fun and merriment— more like the parties we know today than the somber celebration in Wales. On All Souls' Day, November 2, the poor in England walked from door to door begging for food. The custom was called "going a-souling." When people gave the poor special sweets, they promised in return to say prayers for those of the family who had died.

As the years passed, more children than adults went around on All Souls' Day, seeking apples, buns, and money. As they walked the streets of England, they chanted:

> *Soul, soul! for a soul cake!*
> *I pray, good mistress, for a soul cake!*

An apple or a pear, or a plum or a cherry.
Any good thing to make us merry.
One for Peter, two for Paul,
Three for Him Who made us all.
Up with the kettle and down with the pan.
Give us good alms and we'll be gone.

A soul cake was a square bun decorated with currants. It was a special holiday treat that filled bakers' shops just for this one day.

In some countries, like France, people celebrated All Saints' Day (November 1) and All Souls' Day (November 2), but not Halloween (October 31). French bellmen walked through the streets just before midnight on Halloween Eve, warning, "The spirits are about to arrive!" Once they heard this, all hurried to bed and shut their eyes. No one wanted to see these ghostly midnight visitors!

Today on Halloween Eve, French children sometimes beg for flowers with which to decorate churches and the graves of loved ones.

In many lands throughout the world, people still set out special treats for the departed souls. In Mexico, families leave out cakes and toys on Halloween Eve for children who have died. Some parents shoot firecrackers and flares so that the souls of the departed can find their way in the darkness.

All Souls' Day, sometimes called the Day of the Dead, is an important national holiday in Mexico. It's a special time when bakers sell "Dead Men's Bread," baked in the shape of skulls. Children buy toy skeletons and coffins and eat candy skulls, candy coffins, and candy funeral wreaths! It sounds like a strange tradition, but it's all done in good spirits.

In southern Italy, during the fourteenth century, each family prepared a special feast for the souls of the departed on All Souls' Day. In the town of Salerno, it was common to have the family set the table with a bountiful meal. Then all the family members went to church to pray for the souls of the deceased. They stayed there all day, leaving their home open so that the spirits could enter and enjoy the feast.

Woe to the family who returned home to find that their offerings hadn't been consumed. That meant that the spirits disapproved of their home and would work evil against them during the coming year.

Few families returned to find their offerings uneaten though. The practice of setting the banquet table was well known to all the thieves and beggars of Salerno and the surrounding villages. When people left their homes to go to church, the thieves and beggars entered to eat and drink to their hearts' content.

This custom went on for nearly a hundred years. It was finally banned in the fifteenth century by the Church because it was pagan. No doubt the people of Salerno were grateful that they no longer had to cook great dinners for all the local thieves and beggars.

In Ireland, All Hallows' Eve is still a time when ghosts are thought to walk the land and people must be careful to avoid them. The fairies and leprechauns are supposedly out, too, playing tricks on everyone. According to legend, the fairies, though invisible, are always about. In fact, it is still considered bad luck to open a door or a window and throw out the garbage without first telling the fairies to beware. They surely would resent getting their gaily colored clothes soiled by flying garbage!

Many explanations of the origin of fairies have come down to us over the years. One of the most popular is that God made these little creatures on the third day of Creation. But He failed to give them souls. So they must wander the earth until the end of time.

Another belief is that, at the time of the devil's rebellion against God, some angels sided with the devil while others remained true to God. The few who failed to take either side during the battle were cast out and condemned to be fairies on the earth.

In the folklore of fairies, these creatures are immortal. They do not die, as human beings do. But, when Judgment Day comes, they will be destroyed, and good mortal souls will receive eternal life. That is why fairies, while not evil and harmful like witches, are jealous of mortals and like to play tricks on them.

Of course, there are plenty of stories about fairies helping people. Many writers have also created wild tales of mortals who fall in love with and marry fairies and try to help them win a human soul.

Still, people throughout the ages have feared fairies. In Ireland, it was thought that fairies would steal newborn human babies from their cradles and leave fairy children in their place.

Legend says the first
jack-o'-lantern was a turnip
that held a burning chunk
of coal from hell.

Another legend from Ireland concerns the birth of the jack-o'-lantern. According to this tale, an old man named Jack was scurrying home along a country road when the devil suddenly appeared beside him. Jack knew the devil had come to claim his soul, for he had been a stingy, mean, selfish man. As the two walked along, they came to a tree heavy with big, red apples.

"Wouldn't an apple taste good right now?" Jack suggested to the devil.

"They're fine-looking apples, for sure," said the devil. "But they all grow too high for me to reach."

"Then stand on my shoulders," Jack said. "Surely you'll be able to reach them, then."

So the devil climbed up onto Jack's shoulders, swung himself onto a branch of the tree, and began picking the biggest, reddest fruit he could find. Suddenly, Jack whipped out his pocketknife and carved the sign of the cross on the trunk. That made it impossible for the devil to climb down out of the tree.

"Get me down from here," cried the devil, "and I won't claim your soul for ten years!"

But Jack was far too smart to fall for that. "I'll let you down only if you promise *never* to claim my soul," he said. And the devil, desperate to get down, agreed.

But Jack wasn't as smart as he'd thought. Before the next Halloween, his body wore out, and his soul needed a place to go. He was turned back from the gates of heaven because of his stingy, mean ways on earth. When he got to hell, the devil shouted, "Go away! You tricked me into promising I'd never claim your soul. I must keep my word. You cannot enter into hell!"

"But where then shall I go?" Jack asked.

"Back from where you came," the devil replied.

"I'll never find my way back to earth in the dark," Jack cried. So the devil threw him a chunk of coal from the very furnaces of hell. Jack caught the glowing ember and placed it inside a turnip he was gnawing on. He has been wandering the earth with this first jack-o'-lantern in search of a resting place ever since!

3

A WITCH,
A CAT,
AND THINGS
LIKE THAT

Nothing else says Halloween quite like a witch mounted on a broomstick with a black cat perched behind her. She's dressed in flowing black robes and a long pointed cap. Her long, crooked, sinister-looking nose carves an evil silhouette against the evening sky. She is the perfect symbol of evil and mischief.

Nowadays, we laugh at witches. We're used to seeing them in cartoons, on television, in the theater, in comic movies, and on paper decorations. It's all a fun part of the Halloween tradition.

But once, not so very long ago, witches were no laughing matter. Children did not dress up like witches, and adults did not make fun of their costumes.

Hundreds of years ago, most American colonists firmly believed in Satan (the devil) and his helpers. The sermons of the early Puritan preachers were often filled with fiery warn-

*This flying witch can be seen
every year suspended above a roadside
stand near Setauket, New York.*

ings to avoid the tricks of the devil and his servants, witches, warlocks, and imps, who were believed to roam the countryside at night.

Many of the people of New England were terrified of these demons. In fact, a Pilgrim woman named Dinah Sylvester accused the wife of William Holmes, one of Miles Standish's lieutenants, of being a witch. Dinah swore in court that the woman had changed herself into a bear and attacked her. The judge hearing the case ruled against Dinah. He fined her five pounds and ordered her to be whipped for creating such a tale.

Still, it was only a matter of time until an accused witch was found guilty. It happened in Boston in 1648, and the first execution for witchcraft followed. Two years later, the Connecticut colony hanged a witch.

In 1692 in Salem, Massachusetts, witch hunting reached a frightening climax in the Salem Witch Hunt. By the time it had ended, hundreds of innocent people had been accused of practicing witchcraft. Twenty were found guilty and executed.

One Salem woman was accused of being a witch simply because she had baked an apple dumpling. How could the woman get the apple inside the dumpling unless she knew black magic the townspeople asked. The woman was smart enough, however, to make an apple dumpling in court for all to see. After the judge and jury saw how she did this "amazing" thing, she was declared innocent of witchcraft and set free.

The practice of witchcraft was common thousands of years ago in Egypt and later during the early days of the Roman Empire. Eventually, laws were passed forbidding people to destroy crops, pull down crosses and other religious objects, dig

*A witchcraft trial
in Salem, Massachusetts,
in 1692*

up dead bodies, and make images to be used in the rituals of witches and demons.

If a sudden death or illness occurred, though, many people immediately suspected witchcraft. The failure of crops might also be blamed on the curse of some witch. Often, innocent people with strange or unusual habits were charged with the crime of practicing witchcraft and put to death.

Many people believed that witches, who got their unholy powers directly from Satan, could take the form of animals to hide their true identity. Some people accused witches of marrying demons and bringing monster children into the world.

Witches were thought to gather twice each year. Their first meeting was on April 30, the eve before May day. The evening was called *Roodmas* in England and *Walpurgis Night* in Germany. The other great meeting was on the night of October 31, All Hallows' Eve or the Night of Witches. At these times, witches, warlocks, and other creatures of the devil were said to dance around great roaring fires. Before daybreak, they would hop on their brooms and zoom back to their homes—but not before they had planned the mischief and evil they would perform during the coming year.

Witches were known for their magic spells. Often, before their evil deeds could work, they had to brew giant caldrons of the foulest potions imaginable. William Shakespeare, the English writer, described such a brew in the play *Macbeth*. In one scene, three witches work around a boiling caldron chanting:

> *"Double, double toil and trouble;*
> *Fire burn and caldron, bubble.*
> *Fillet of a feeny snake,*

In the caldron boil and bake;
Eye of newt, and toe of frog,
Wool of bat, and tongue of dog,
Adder's fork, and blind-worm's sting,
Lizard's leg, and howlet's wing—
For a charm of powerful trouble,
Like a hell-broth boil and bubble."

Do you want to meet a witch face to face? According to tradition, there is an easy way. On Halloween Eve, put your clothes on inside out. Then walk backward to a crossroads. As the clock strikes midnight, a witch will appear at your side.

Of course, that's all fantasy. People today know there are no witches. But hundreds of years ago superstitions often got the better of people. Not only were witches to be avoided, but also their most frequent companions, black cats. During the great witch hunts in Europe and America during the seventeenth century, cats were often tortured and killed. That is because it was believed they were the soulmates of witches.

No one is certain how cats came to be associated with witches and demons. Possibly it is their sinister look, their aloofness, or the green glare of their eyes. Both dogs and cats have been thought to possess ESP. But while it's said that dogs curl up their tails and slowly slink away in the presence of the supernatural, cats are quite at home with it.

Not only did witches and devils have cats as companions, they were supposed to be able to change themselves into cats as well. Since no one knew whether a cat was harmless or a witch in disguise, all cats were suspected of being connected with evil.

In Ireland, people thought cats were associated with the devil. So, if a traveler encountered a cat during a journey and

the cat stared him or her in the face, the person thought better of continuing. The look of the demon cat surely meant bad luck. To this day many people still refuse to cross the path of a black cat because of this superstition.

One famous story, told in many versions throughout northern England, tells of the cat's supernatural powers. A man reading a book in front of the fireplace one night heard a sudden noise in the chimney. As he looked on, a cat appeared in the fireplace. It leaped across the burning logs into the room and cried out, "Tell Dildrum that Doldrum is dead!" Then, with a leap and a yowl, the cat disappeared up the chimney.

The man, startled by what he'd seen, called to his wife. She came running into the room, followed by the family cat. After the husband told the wife what had happened, their usually well-behaved pet suddenly raised up and exclaimed, "So Doldrum is dead!" And it then leaped across the fire and up the chimney—never to be seen again.

Doldrum, it turns out, was King of all Catland. Dildrum, who had been living quietly for years as the family's housecat, left to take his place on the throne.

With tall tales like that, is it any wonder that witches and cats are among the most popular Halloween superstitions?

4

TRICK OR TREAT?

Today in the United States and other countries around the world, the eve of October 31 means one thing to millions of youngsters: Trick or Treat. The custom of dressing up in costumes and going around the neighborhood seeking special Halloween treats is fairly new, but the traditions behind trick-or-treating go back centuries.

The source of the trick-or-treating custom is probably ancient Ireland. There, on the night of October 31, the peasants paraded from house to house in search of contributions to Muck Olla, a Druid god.

This ancient procession was led by a man wearing a white robe and a horsehead mask. (The horse was sacred, a symbol of fertility, to the Druid's sun god.) The leader was called Lair Bhan, which means white mare. Behind him walked the young men who served as his assistants, blowing cows' horns to let the villagers know they were coming. Others followed the group throughout the evening, sometimes making a procession of fifty people or more.

At each farmhouse the costumed leader called out the head of the household. Then he recited a long string of verses that told the farmer that his good fortunes were due to the goodness of Muck Olla. So, if the farmer wanted to prosper during the coming year, he had better make a generous contribution to that spirit.

That was usually enough to make the farmer open up his heart and his purse strings to Muck Olla. If not, Lair Bhan issued a dire warning of what might happen if Muck Olla's messengers were not treated well. There might be famine or drought. The farmer's family might suffer great illness or death. His animals might die. His crop yields might be too small to see his family through the coming year. Few farmers wanted to deal with the vengeance of an angry Muck Olla. So, nearly all gave generously. Then the procession staggered happily home with such offerings as butter, eggs, corn, and potatoes. Some rich farmers even gave gold coins.

Not all of the tradition of "dressing up" on Halloween comes from pagan ritual though. It also has its origins in the Roman Catholic Church, the main church of Ireland. On All Hallows, many churches staged plays called *pageants* for the benefit of their members. Those in the pageant dressed up as the *patron saints* who were their special guardians. Those who were not playing the parts of holy ones also got into the act by dressing up as devils. The All Hallows procession marched from the church out to the churchyard, where the play often continued until late evening. In time, nearly everyone in Ireland thought of October 31 as a night for dressing up in costume—either to satisfy the pagan god, Muck Olla, or as part of the Christian ceremony of All Hallows.

Gradually, the costumes of Halloween changed from the traditional horses, saints, and devils to ghosts, witches, and goblins. Some people hoped that dressing in scary costumes would trick demons prowling the earth on Halloween into thinking they were demons, too. Then the real demons would leave them alone. Others felt that scary costumes might frighten away creatures from the world of Satan.

Eventually, the custom of dressing up in costume and the custom of going from house to house in search of "treats" were combined. In England, the custom of searching for treats probably goes back to the tradition of "a-souling," or begging for cakes for the dead. Youngsters dressed in costumes traveled from door to door, crying "Treats for the goblins" or "Trick or treat?" If they received a treat the youngsters moved merrily on to the next door. If not, they performed a trick.

From time to time, Halloween tricks got out of hand. Around 1900, when outside restrooms called "outhouses" were still commonly used in rural areas, Halloween tricksters often upturned them or carried them off. Sometimes, they set fire to the outhouses, burning them to the ground. They thought it was great fun to see the owners come out to use the restroom, only to find it gone.

Today, in order to prevent such tricks and to make trick-or-treating safer, some communities in the United States require that adults go door to door with children. A few communities have even banned the custom of trick-or-treating. Instead, schools, civic groups, and community groups hold parties, costume balls, or contests. There, the wearer of the most creative costume wins a prize. Children also bob for apples and tell ghost stories.

Unfortunately, many boys and girls around the world aren't able to enjoy Halloween. In fact, many children have

*The money raised from trick-or-treating
for UNICEF is used to help
children in developing countries.*

barely enough food to eat and clothes to keep them warm. In order to help these less fortunate children, many youngsters go trick-or-treating for the United Nations International Children's Fund, or UNICEF.

Instead of seeking candy, cookies, and chewing gum for themselves, UNICEF trick-or-treaters ask for donations of money. This buys food, medicine, and other goods for poor children around the world.

You can join the yearly trick-or-treat for UNICEF program. For more information write to the United States Committee for UNICEF, 331 E. 38th Street, New York, NY 10016. You'll have fun dressing up and going trick-or-treating. At the same time, you'll be helping those less fortunate than you.

Be sure to get your parents' permission before you do any kind of trick-or-treating.

Whatever we do on Halloween, all of us believe an old superstition or two. We may not be bothered by a black cat crossing our paths. We may not believe that ghosts will visit our homes in search of great feasts. But who would dare venture out alone on Halloween night to walk through a graveyard?

Witches? Ghosts? Goblins? We all know they don't exist. Or do we?

5

HAVING A
HALLOWEEN
PARTY

Chills and thrills—it's Halloween night, when witches fly and goblins prowl. It's also a wonderful night to throw a party. You can make your Halloween party as spooky as ever. And you can start by making your own Halloween party invitations.

First decide how many people you want to invite to your party. Then go to an art supply store, dimestore, or department store that sells construction paper. Orange paper is good for pumpkin invitations and black paper is good for witches' caldron invitations. Each sheet of 8 × 10 inch (20 × 25 cm) paper will make three invitations.

To make the invitations, first fold the sheets of construction paper into thirds. Then cut along the fold marks. Each sheet should give you three strips measuring roughly 3 1/3 × 8 inches (8 × 20 cm). Don't worry if the strips aren't all exactly the same size.

Next, take the strips, one at a time, and fold them in half so they resemble cards. Using a soft-lead pencil, make the outline of a pumpkin or a caldron on the front of each card. Then cut each figure out with blunt-nosed scissors. Make sure you don't cut along the folded edges. You should end up with hinged pumpkins or caldrons.

Use a felt-tipped marker to draw a face on the front of each pumpkin. Write a message inside each card, such as: "Let's celebrate Halloween. Come to a party at Don and Rick's house. Drop by at 8 P.M. on October 31." Include your address and any other necessary information.

On the black-paper caldron invitations, the writing must be light so the message will show up. Use a pen and white ink or a thin paintbrush and white water-based paint.

Once your invitations are complete, you can hand them out to your friends. Or you can slip them into envelopes, address them, and put them in the mail. They should fit into a small envelope with room to spare. Be sure to put on the right postage.

Once the invitations have been sent out, start working on the party decorations. You may want to tape a store-bought pumpkin, witch, or skeleton to the front door. Or, you may want to have some fun making your own decorations.

You can cut out various Halloween shapes from construction paper and tape them to the walls or hang them from the lights by thread. Black witches and cats, orange pumpkins, and green moons are all terrific holiday cutouts.

Do you want to make your party room really eerie? Find some small sections of dead tree branches and paint them white. Using fine thread and thumbtacks or tape, hang the painted branches from the ceiling. Make string spider webs, moss made from gray crepe paper, and a few construction paper cutouts to hang from the branches. Then see how spine-chilling it looks when the lights are turned low!

You can buy many types of party favors and table settings for Halloween. But you can make really great pumpkin party favors yourself. All you need are orange crepe paper, some Halloween candies, and small pieces of string, twist-ems, or rubber bands.

For each favor lay out several pieces of Halloween candy on a 6-inch (15-cm) crepe paper square. Then gather all four corners of the paper together at the top, creating a ball filled with candy. Fasten the corners together with string, twist-ems, or rubber bands. Then take a felt-tipped marker and draw the eyes, nose, and mouth on your orange ball. You now have a pumpkin favor.

You can use white glue to attach some dried oak leaves to the bottom of your paper pumpkin favor. Or tape several cutout paper leaves to the bottom for a dressy effect. Make sure you have a pumpkin favor for everyone at the party. Perhaps you might even want to make some extras to use as prizes for the winners of your party games.

Many of the Halloween games that are popular at parties today have been played for years. In England and pioneer America, Halloween was often called *Snap Apple Night* or *Nut-crack Night*. That is because it came at the time of year when both apples and nuts had matured and were brought in, to the delight of the entire family.

One of the most popular of all games was bobbing for apples, and it is still popular today. This game is played with a large tub of water and several more apples than players. The apples are floated in about 12 inches (30 cm) of water. Each player must grab an apple from the water in order to win. The player who gets the apple in the shortest time is the winner.

The only catch is that players can't use their hands. The apples must be grabbed with the teeth!

To make the game more interesting, place a time limit of a minute or two on each player. To lengthen the game, you can play two or three rounds. At the end of all the rounds, each player's times are added up. The player with the shortest total time is the winner.

Several other games that were popular in England and during pioneer days involved telling fortunes. One of the best-loved of all was one in which two nuts were placed in a burning fireplace. Each nut was named for a friend. If one nut cracked and jumped away, the spirits were supposedly warning that the friend the nut represented was not true. The nut that burned with a steady glow stood for the true friend. Of course, if both nuts jumped away, there was likely to be quite a bit of laughter and teasing. There may even have been a few suggestions that the person taking the "test" find new friends.

Apples, too, were used in early America to predict the future. You supposedly could tell a person's "true love" by giving him or her an apple and a small paring knife or apple peeler. The person was told to cut round and round the apple, until a long, continuous peel was removed. Then this person closed his or her eyes and swung the peel overhead three times, chanting, "By this peel let me discover the initial letter of my true lover." Next, the person would throw the peel over his or her left shoulder. When it fell to the ground, it was supposed to form the first letter of the name of that person's true love.

Burning nuts in
England around 1886

Sometimes it was not easy to read an "A" for Abigail or an "S" for Steve out of a squiggly length of peeling! But it *was* fun!

Still a third old game to come from pioneer times is called "The Three Luggies." To play, you first set out three clean bowls on a table. Place an apple in one and a nut in the other. The third bowl can be filled with soot or ashes, or left empty. Blindfold each player in the game one at a time, and spin the player around twice. Then tell him or her to reach into one of the bowls. The bowl with the apple might stand for good luck, wealth, or love. The bowl with the nut might mean things will continue pretty much unchanged. The empty or soot-filled bowl might stand for sickness, the loss of a girlfriend or boyfriend, or failing a subject in school.

Still another future-predicting test popular in the 1800s was "Throwing the Shoe." One of the participants would remove his or her shoe and fling it high up in the air, often over the roof of the family cabin. If the shoe came to rest pointing *toward* the house, it meant the person taking the test would stay home during the coming year. If the shoe pointed *away*, that meant there was travel in the future. And if the shoe landed with the bottom facing up, it meant bad luck was on the way.

You can play the same shoe game—outdoors, of course. But don't try throwing it over your house unless your parents have a ladder and are willing to climb up on the roof to get the shoe!

From the American Indians comes something fun to make on Halloween. The Indians used devices called *wind-paddle moaners* in many of their ceremonial dances. The paddles made weird moaning noises when whirled rapidly through the air. Some said they sounded like the moans of a ghost.

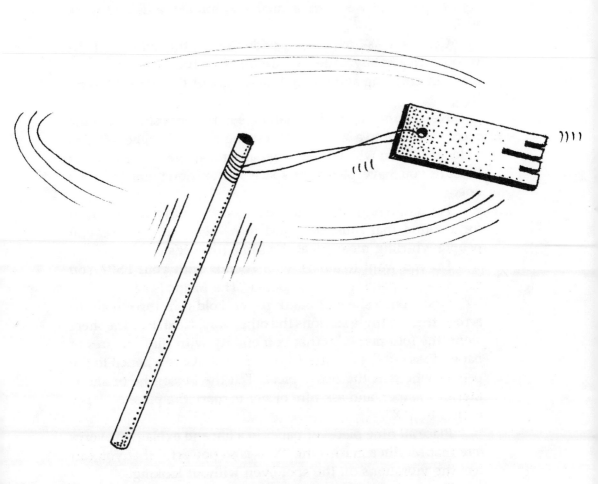

WIND PADDLE MOANER

To make one, you first need a thin piece of wood about 7 inches (18 cm) long and 2 inches (5 cm) wide. Cedar shakes or similar pieces of wood are available at lumberyards and work well.

Cut three 1/8-inch (.3-cm)-wide slots in the tail end of the wood with a hobby knife. Be careful! Make the outer two slots 1 inch (2.5 cm) long and the middle slot about 1 3/4 inches (4.5 cm) long.

Next, punch or drill a small hole in the opposite end of the piece. Attach it to a stick, using a string about 18 inches (46 cm) in length. Then whirl the moaner around above your head, but be sure you have plenty of space so you don't smack someone.

For a different sound, make a moaner with five slits. And for a sound that must be heard to be believed, have several people whirling moaners at the same time. It's *eerie!*

Do you want to amaze your friends with your ESP? You can do it by playing a game called "The Magic Spot."

First, take a sheet of blank paper. Fold it in three sections across, then in three sections the other way. Next, tear the sheet along the fold marks so that you end up with nine squares of paper. Pass out the squares to your friends. Give a pencil to the person who gets the *center* piece. Tell the person he or she is Merlin's helper, and ask him or her to mark the piece of paper with a big "X".

Place all nine pieces of paper in a hat and explain to everyone that Merlin's mark—the "X"—is so powerful that you can feel the vibrations on the spot even without looking.

To prove it, have someone blindfold you. Then stir the pieces of paper with your hand for several moments. Finally, pull out the piece with the Magic Spot!

How do you do this fantastic magic trick? It's easy. All the pieces of paper you tore will have at least one smooth edge—except for the center piece. That will have jagged edges on all four sides. That, of course, is the piece with the Magic Spot on it. When you feel it in the hat, simply pull it out, mumbling something about the powerful energy waves it's giving off. You will be sure to mystify your friends!

6

MAKING A
HALLOWEEN
COSTUME

There are costume shops that rent costumes of various characters—both real and imaginary—to people who want to dress up on Halloween. But these costumes can cost a lot. One shop charges over $200 to rent a Star Wars costume for one night!

You're not likely to spend $200 on a Halloween costume. But even if you *did* have that kind of money, you wouldn't have as much fun renting a costume as you'd have making it yourself. Think of how proud you'll be when someone says, "Wow, really neat! Where did you get your costume?"

Making your own costume can be as difficult or as easy as you like. If one of your parents or someone you know is experienced in sewing or design, you may want to ask him or her to help you make a fancy costume. But there are simple-to-make costumes that are creative and fun to put together.

Probably the simplest make-it-yourself costume is the ghost. Take an old, unwanted, white sheet and drape it over yourself. Then have someone mark the places where your eyes and nose touch the sheet with a felt-tipped marker. Remove the sheet. Using blunt scissors, carefully cut out a hole for each eye and a breathing hole.

To keep the sheet from slipping around as you walk, wear a tight-fitting old hat over the top of the sheet. Be sure the sheet is trimmed at the bottom so it is at least 6 inches (15 cm) from the floor. Otherwise, you may step on it and trip as you walk.

Another simple costume is that of a bum or tramp. You'll need some old, ragged clothes (add a few extra rips here and there), some soot for dirt, and a few scrap cloth patches, to be either sewn on or attached with safety pins. A pair of pants two or three sizes too large for you is ideal. Roll up the cuffs so that you don't trip on them, and pin them up so they don't slip down as you're walking. Find an old piece of rope to tie around your waist like a belt. That should keep the pants up above your hips, where they belong.

Wear an oversized shirt and roll up the sleeves. Some soot from a freshly burned candle, a little dirt, or some dark mascara applied here and there to your face will help complete the look you want. Top your wardrobe off with old shoes and a floppy hat.

Sometimes you can make several different costumes from clothing you have on hand. If you already own a cowboy hat, you'll need little more to complete a cowboy costume. A brown paper bag opened up and cut so that it lies flat can serve as "chaps," or leggings. Cut the bag lengthwise down the middle until you have two equal pieces about 3 feet (.9 m) long. Along one edge, cut small slits to resemble fringe. Do the same with the other "chap." Then safety-pin the chaps to your pants, with the fringe sticking out on each side.

Add a hat, a scarf (which can be a handkerchief tied loosely around your neck), and perhaps a rope coiled to look like a lariat. Now you're in business.

Of course, many people enjoy wearing masks for Halloween and seeing if others can guess who they are. You can do this, too, and you need not buy an expensive mask. You can make nearly any mask you want with just a little thought and creativity.

Find a brown paper bag that's in good condition. If there is printing on the bag, turn it inside out. Place the bag over your head and trim it for the proper length. It should rest comfortably on your shoulders, with the top of your head against the inside bottom of the bag. Ask a friend to help so it fits properly.

Find the spots for the eye holes. Remove the bag and, using blunt scissors, cut the holes out. Make them large enough so that when the bag shifts to one side or the other, you'll still be able to see out.

Finally, decorate the "face" of the bag with felt-tipped markers. Add some crepe paper or construction paper cutout features such as ears, whiskers, a nose, and a tongue, and your mask is complete.

Here are hints for making some other simple Halloween costumes.

Cat. Make a paper-bag mask that resembles a cat's head. Wear lightweight black pajamas or leotards over your clothes. Ask one of your parents to sew a rope "tail," dyed black, to the back of the pajama bottoms. To complete the outfit, wear a pair of black sneakers or basketball shoes with "claws" painted on with water-based paints.

Pumpkin. Use a paper-bag mask covered with orange crepe paper (apply the paper with white glue) or painted with orange water-based paint. The back of the mask should be longer than the front so that you can glue large, green cutout construction-paper leaves to it. If you like, you can trail several leaves down your back so that they look like a cape. Or circle them around your shoulders and attach them in front to form a neckpiece.

Witch. For this costume, you'll need some makeup. Use a white base to make your face look ghostly. Ruby-red lipstick to highlight your mouth and dark eyeshadow to highlight your eyes will complete the look. You can roll a sheet of black construction paper into a cone for a hat. Use several sheets of black crepe paper glued together to form a black skirt and cape. Carry a broom, preferably an old, ratty-looking one.

Goblin. Wear a paper-bag mask covered with light-green crepe paper (apply the paper with white glue) or painted light green with water-based paint. Add some elfish-looking ears made of black construction paper, and wear an orange paper hat and bathrobe.

Pirate. Make a black construction-paper eye patch fastened to a piece of elastic. Be sure the elastic isn't too tight. Tie a colorful scarf around your head, add a sash around your waist, and carry a heavy cardboard sword in your sash. Complete the outfit by adding a dark mascara "scar" or two to your cheeks.

PAPER BAG MASK

ROBOT COSTUME

Robot. Make a paper-bag mask sprayed with metallic silver paint. For antennae, use extra-long pipe cleaners, which you can purchase at most dime and novelty stores. Curl the cleaners by wrapping them tightly around a pencil. Then remove them and stretch them out slightly. Attach the cleaners to the top or sides of the mask with clear tape or silver duct tape.

Next, take a large cardboard box and cut a hole in the bottom through which your head will fit. Cut an armhole in each side and slip the box on. Once you know it fits, you can decorate the box by gluing aluminum foil to the outside or spraying it silver. Add various buttons, spools, and other small gizmos for "controls." Complete the outfit with white leotards and tennis shoes.

7

THINGS THAT GO BUMP IN THE NIGHT

With ghosts and goblins about on Halloween, it's only natural that plenty of strange tales have come down to us throughout time. Some of them, of course, are sheer fantasy, made up to amuse others on the night of the unearthly. But other tales, people swear, are true.

This tale supposedly happened more than a hundred years ago. A salesman who was traveling far from home was surprised to see his sister pass him going the other way. He called out to her, but she didn't answer. He turned to go after her, but she had ducked into an alleyway and disappeared.

When the salesman returned home, he told his mother of the strange incident. The mother, in tears, said that what he thought he saw was impossible, for the man's sister had died suddenly just a few days before. The salesman was heartbroken, of course. Still, he was puzzled by the incident. Several days later, while dining with his mother, the man mentioned the

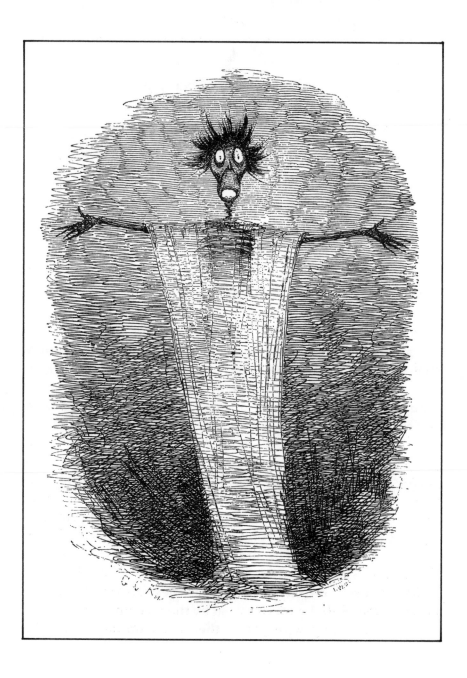

incident again. He said he had noticed a small scratch on the cheek of the girl he thought was his sister. Suddenly, his mother began to cry, and he went to comfort her.

"What's the matter?" he asked. "I realize now that the girl I saw couldn't have been Marie."

The mother shook her head and looked at her son. She explained to him that while preparing the body for the funeral, she had accidentally made just such a scratch! She had carefully covered the scratch with makeup so that no one else knew of its existence!

Ghosts frequently are said to appear to dying people, as if to welcome them to another life after death. One story tells of a Mrs. Blank, who was near death. She reported that she had seen a vision of a beautiful young girl, whom the family had known six years earlier. Mrs. Blank's relatives told her that the girl was living far away, and that her vision was nothing more than a dream. But later the family received word that the girl Mrs. Blank had seen had mysteriously died just eleven days earlier.

Each year, there are thousands of reports of ghosts and ghostly happenings in the United States alone. Some incidents may be due to overactive imaginations, while others are much more difficult to explain.

Take some of the bizarre incidents which have occurred at Whaley House in San Diego, California, for instance. More than a century ago, Whaley House was the scene of much tragedy. Sickness, death, and cruel treatment seemed to plague

*A wood engraving of
a ghostly apparition*

the Whaley family. Today, the home is a historical landmark and a museum open to the public. The curator of Whaley House is convinced it is also one of the most actively haunted houses in the country!

One day, while the curator was upstairs working on some papers, she heard beautiful music coming from the drawing room, where the old piano which Mrs. Whaley had once played was located. Thinking that some guests had entered the home and started playing, the curator went downstairs to greet them. Imagine her surprise when she found not guests, but Mrs. Whaley! She was seated at the piano wearing her favorite dress—the dress she'd worn when she sat for an oil painting more than a century ago. The curator stared in amazement as the figure at the piano played for several moments. Then, suddenly, it vanished.

Several months later, while walking up the stairs to the upper living quarters, the curator was frightened by the figure of a man coming down. She recognized the man from historical descriptions. She froze, startled, as Mr. Whaley descended, then walked *through* her, and finally disappeared!

On still another occasion, the curator was checking the house for lingering guests before closing time. As she went from room to room, she felt a spine-chilling coldness about her, as though an icy draft had just blown through. Yet, it was the middle of summer, all the windows were closed, and there was no air conditioning. The chill grew worse as the curator reached the doorway to the room that had been used by the

The ghosts of
two dead persons

Whaley's young daughter. Long before, the girl had taken ill and died unexpectedly. When the curator looked into the room, she saw Mrs. Whaley sitting at the foot of the girl's bed. The woman seemed to be examining some clothing. After several moments, the figure changed into a ball of light and disappeared. The chill vanished with her.

With all our advanced technology and scientific methods, we still cannot explain incidents like those above. But it seems that ghosts or spirits, if they exist at all, are harmless. They may frighten people, but there has never been proof that a spirit has actually harmed anyone.

Of course, that's not what tall tales and ghost stories which have been passed down to us over the years would have us believe. Several master storytellers are famous for spinning yarns of spirits, ghosts, goblins, and the like. Edgar Allen Poe, an American writer who lived from 1809 to 1849, wrote what are probably some of the most terrifying stories ever. They include such tales as *The Fall of the House of Usher* and *The Telltale Heart*. Washington Irving, another American writer, who lived from 1783 to 1859, certainly had fun writing about the unexplainable in his tales *Rip Van Winkle* and *The Legend of Sleepy Hollow*.

Then there are other lesser-known tales. Many are obviously fantasy, but they are still scary. One is the folktale of *The Man and His Bride*.

A long time ago in a place since forgotten, a man in his mid-thirties married a beautiful young woman. He was a very successful businessman and banker. She was a wonderful companion and homemaker.

One of the things that the man liked about his wife was the way she dressed. She wore only the finest gowns and skirts, and her shoes were always spotless. Her hair was per-

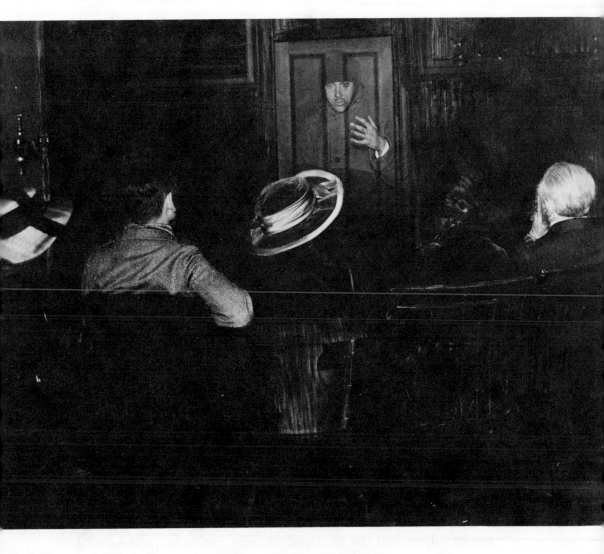

*Photograph of a supposed
apparition during a seance
around 1910*

fectly arranged upon her head, no matter what time of day or night.

After several weeks of a very happy marriage, the husband commented upon how lovely his wife always looked.

"Thank you," she replied. "It's nice of you to say so."

Several more weeks passed, and the man noticed that his new bride, who never wore the same dress twice, always wore the same black satin ribbon around her neck. Curious, he asked her about it. Her only reply was, "Don't ever touch my ribbon."

The man let the matter drop for a while. Eventually, though, he grew more and more curious about the ribbon. Why would a woman who never wore the same dress twice always wear the same black ribbon?

Finally, when they were seated at dinner one evening, the man said half-jokingly, "Dear, if you don't take that ribbon off soon, I'm going to take it off for you."

The woman grew very pale, and her eyes took on a stern look. "Don't do that," she said firmly. In her voice was a tone the man had never heard before, and he was genuinely frightened.

Several more days passed, and the man had become more curious than ever. One evening, as he settled into bed with his wife, he demanded that she remove the ribbon. "Do it now," he said, "or I shall do it for you."

Once again, the woman took on a strange, faraway look before saying sternly, "Don't do that."

With that stern warning, she turned over and was soon sound asleep. But the husband, determined to learn the secret of the ribbon, could not rest until he removed it from her neck. Slowly, carefully, he moved close to her. Very cautiously, he reached out to unclasp the gold pin which held the ribbon tight. But when his fingers touched it, he yelped with pain. The pin was as hot as a coal from the fireplace!

The man looked at his fingers, which were burned and aching as though they had touched fire. But he was determined to remove that ribbon! So he got up from bed, went to his wife's sewing basket, and found a pair of scissors. Slowly and quietly so as not to awaken her, he crept up on her, placing one edge of the scissors against her neck and gently working the blade beneath the ribbon. Then, with one quick movement, he snipped the ribbon in two.

Imagine his surprise when the ribbon fell free—and his wife's head popped off her shoulders. It rolled down to the floor, where it bounced halfway across the room, leaving tiny pools of blood in its path!

From the wife's lips came the stern reminder, "I... told ... you ... not ... to ... do that!"

INDEX